Designed To Testify

Katandra Jackson Nunnally

Printed in the United States of America

Cover design by Elaina Lee
Final Edit by Danielle Bell

First Printing, 2016

 ISBN 978-0986100192

FreedomInk Publishing
P O Box 1093
Reidsville, Georgia 30453
www.freedomink365.com

1. Religion : Christian Life - Personal Growth

2. Religion : Christian Life - Spiritual Growth

I dedicate this book to my Grandfathers who art in Heaven:

Randall Jackson & William Edward Byrd.

I'll see you when I get there...

Foreword

The most important decision a person can make is deciding whether or not GOD is real. The hardest decision a person will ever make is deciding to follow HIM. Make no mistake, being a Christian is the best decision one could ever make because you enjoy the peace of knowing that HE is the captain of your life and HE controls your destiny. However, being a Christian does not exempt you from troubles, trials, or temptations. You can't be a saint unless you acknowledge that you were once a sinner. It is the struggles that we all go through that mature our faith in Christ and grow our relationship with HIM. Every day we are faced with temptations and one of the biggest misconceptions of being a Christian is that you are immune to temptations just because you are "saved". One must remember that Christ saves your spirit not your body. In other words, your spirit is saved but your flesh is always lost and as a result it is continuously at war with your spirit every single day. It is only by the Blood of Jesus Christ that we are able to overcome the enemy and it is through that experience which produces our testimony (Rev 12:11).

The NEW Testament is filled with many miracles that Jesus wrought, from making the lame to walk and the dumb to talk, from healing issues to healing infirmities, yet HIS only stipulation was for those who were healed to go show the world what HE had done and what HE could do if only they believe. Perhaps you don't have a testimony as radical as the woman with the issue of blood (Luke 8:43) but whatever HE has delivered you from or is delivering you from, we have a responsibility to "tell the story" of what HE has done for us. Our prayer is that this book will serve as a motivation to continue your walk in Christ as a Believer and if you are not a Christian hopefully this book will inspire you to accept Christ, the only ONE who can take a mess and turn it into a masterpiece; an instrument that is truly designed to testify!

Reverend Brandon Lewis

Disclaimer

The composition of this book is not to answer every question that may arise in regards to the subject matter at hand. Neither is it intended to go into great depth. Something as intimate as religion and establishing a one on one relationship with God (if that is something that you desire), should be a personal journey. The purpose of this book is to:

Offer courage— You are brave.

Jumpstart a conversation. Be it dialogue between many, or as few as just you— Take it to the Lord, and you'll never converse alone.

Encourage and enhance your journey— Biblical examples have been set before us. Physical examples have been set before us. Personal accounts, like this one, have been made readily available.

My prayer is that this book will serve as a turning point in your journey. Seek ye the Kingdom of God for yourself, so that others will recognize His goodness when they see you, and choose to seek Him too.

Special Thanks

To my husband, Jeremy— Thank you for being the best travel partner ever! It doesn't matter if we're driving to the corner store or clear across the country. Or if we're taking a leisure stroll or coming to the most important conclusion in life, God is real! Every step of this journey has been even more amazing because you're by my side. I can't wait to get those Passports. Where shall we go?

To my children, Jermaine 'Tre', Kailyn Elise & Ashley Vanique— Thanks y'all for always keeping momma on her toes. Amidst the chaos of life, I have had the extreme privilege of raising you three and preparing you for the world. As much as you've learned from me over the years, I've learned from each of you.

To a few very special friends, Jamie Arnold & Rita Forest— Thank you for your friendship & your love. Your support continues to fan the flames of my wildest dreams. Keep reading and I'll keep writing!

To my church family, First African Missionary Baptist Church in Claxton GA— Thank you for accepting me & my family. I know I may seem a bit quiet and a bit reserved, but my heart is overwhelmed to be a member of your house & a part of God's Family.

To my mother, Vernice Byrd Scott— Thank you for standing in the gap for me. Thank you for praying for me.

Saving the best for last, Alpha & Omega— I know that You are God all by Yourself and You don't need any help from me. But You still chose to use me. I am in awe of Your greatness. I am astounded by Your mercy & grace. I am blown away by Your unending, never wavering, unconditional love for me. Beyond Your affections for me, I thank You for being You.

It took weathering the storm, surviving the rain and finally coming to a place of absolute tranquility for me to understand that no testimony is in vain.

Take Me.

I'm Yours.

Here I am, standing at a crossroad, straddling the fence so to speak. A solemn limbo somewhere in between sinner and saint. Ready to live right and fully give my life to Jesus Christ, but afraid of what that might mean! Must I trade my blue jeans and tees for dresses and skirts? Am I to denounce the world? And is that even possible? How can I separate myself from something that I am very much a part of? Are Christians allowed to have fun or is it strictly a mission to be about God's business and God's business only? Once I say "I do" just how will my life change after promising myself to that life altering commitment? What happens after I submit myself willingly unto the mercy of the alter? What does it mean to be born again? Is being baptized an absolute necessity? I can't swim and the thought of being submersed under water at the hands of another completely unnerves me! Just what does it mean to be saved anyway? How does one become saved? I have so many questions, concerns, doubts and uncertainties... But I've gotten way ahead of myself.

Jesus, I humbly come before You, asking that You guide me so that I may find the path of righteousness that You've so graciously set before me. I desire an intimate relationship with our Heavenly Father and it is YOU whom lights the way.

John 14:6 -- Jesus answered, "I am the way and the truth and the life. No one comes to the Father except through me."

My prayer is that the composition of this book will give another the courage to seek for themselves, the Kingdom of Heaven.

In His Image.

A Noble Thing.

The upheaval of the only life I've ever known, and this pending and unknown journey has officially been accepted! I've suffered so much heartache. Harshness has been my reality. Looking back, I never asked why. I just accepted every tribulation as a part of life. Unbeknownst to me, those same trials would become my triumphs. I witnessed someone amazing testify that, "In order to rightfully claim your testimony, you must first endure the test".

Psalm 30:5 -- "For his anger lasts only moment; but his favor lasts a lifetime; weeping may stay for the night, but rejoicing comes in the morning."

If I may set the stage...

I was raised by a single mother, and after being 'legally' abducted, I was molested over the course of several years by an estranged father. Teenage pregnancy. High school drop-out. An unwed teenage mommy, still a kid myself. I engaged in promiscuous behavior as I fully embraced a carnal addiction. I offered sex too freely, too willingly, and hoped for love in return.

I've surrendered my body (and my sanity) to too many back to back relationships and fleeting intimacies. I've dated a woman, once. I've been divorced, twice. I've raised three children, one of whom has a lifelong disability. The fridge has run bare. The vehicle has been repossessed. The electricity has been cut off. I considered turning to cocaine but I suppose hard drugs never did appeal to me. What would become my choice of poison? Scotch on the rocks. Vodka straight. Rum no chaser. The consecrated bottle contained liquid salvation. I've contemplated suicide and entertained constant morbid thoughts! In the face of it all, I never worried, never cried, never asked why. Feeling sorry for myself and giving up has never been an option. I did what was required for me and mine to survive. Somehow I've always known that I would be alright. Somehow I've always known that no hurdle thrown in my path was too large to overcome. But how did I understand a truth that was yet unknown? There is so much blight here on Earth. But this place is only momentary.

Questions.

Unanswered.

What does it mean to be born again?

If Jesus was a Jew, then why strive to be a Christian?

How will I know that I'm ready?

After I'm saved, why is being baptized a separate event?

In what ways will my life change?

Do I have to wear dresses?

What about my tattoos?

I've been divorced? Does that guarantee me a one-way ticket to hell?

Will God truly forgive me for ALL my sins?

Why does Jesus love me? It's never crossed my mind to ask before and maybe I'm wrong for doing so now... But why me?

Is there a such thing as Moral Fatigue? Can one ever get tired of doing the right thing?

Do I have to attend church every Sunday? What now?

I'm a firm believer that there is a divine purpose for our existence. We're not just simply here to be here. Only God knows what we were created for. Who we were created for is the utmost Divine. Our purpose is to uplift, glorify, and magnify His Holy name. Not ourselves, our agendas or our own beliefs! Who really wants to hear this though? It took me a long time to finally take heed & hear these words. I'm listening & watching! The government is getting aligned with end times. Passing laws to pacify mankind. Giving the world permission to do what the Bible clearly punishes.

Romans 12:2 -- Do not conform to the pattern of this world, but be transformed by the renewing of your mind. Then you will be able to test and approve what God's will is--his good, pleasing and perfect will.

Inner Conflict.

Silent Turmoil.

The old me and the new me cannot coexist within the same body. It's time to do some spiritual cleansing. My heart is under construction and this temple is under new management. The new me is the tenant... Father I come to You through Your one and only Son, asking You to take over as the head of my life. It's been You there all along seeing me through those hard days and long nights. I've been so foolish. Now I see the error of my ways. You've walked beside me, You've carried me. A silent stride, Your hand guiding mine and I was unaware. So many miles You've walked for the sake of me. You kept me. Now I am taking that one step towards You. The only step You've ever asked me to take. Please make me over. Make me whole. Make me a new creation. Pleasing to thy sight. So at the end of my days, You will deem me Your worthy and faithful servant.

A spiritual war has been waged. The old me & the new me cannot be friends. What's it going to be? My way and the few, fleeting secular pleasures of the world? Or God's way and the immeasurable pleasure of His love for the rest of eternity?

2 Corinthians 5:17 -- Therefore, if anyone is in Christ, the new creation has come: The old has gone, the new is here!

I choose the new me!

Out with the old.

In with the new.

January 2nd, the first Sunday of the new year. The previous year came to a close with uncertainties laid to rest. I was ready. Assured that a stack of Bibles crashing down on me from the heavens would not be the sign, I was to look inward, to the very core of my heart. If this walk with Christ was for me, I would know when the time came. After sitting in church for a month of Sundays, I had come to several conclusions. One of which was the revelation that there definitely would be no stack of Bibles.

If I may backtrack a bit... Several weeks before I confessed with my mouth that I believe in my heart, that Christ is my Savior and accepted Him as the head of my new life, I began a journey I had no idea was underfoot.

My mother invited me to attend the 125th anniversary of her church. The presiding Pastor of my mother's church had invited another to deliver the sermon. A guest Pastor. I had no expectations whatsoever. Honestly, I was in attendance simply and merely because I'd been invited.

I was not prepared for what happened next. The conviction in which the sermon was delivered caught me totally by surprise. I had been spiritually reached by a powerful man of God, a Pastor who'd done such a thorough job of penetrating beyond the layers of outer shell, built up by years of pain. So powerful was this man of God, I pressed my way through the congregation after that fateful service. I had to meet the young Pastor and I had to know where his church home was. I've never in all my life been to church back to back, two Sundays in a row. That was the first old decree that I broke.

The following Sunday I was present in the house of the Lord once more. Breaking those unspoken rules that I'd set forth. Lo and behold, the Overseer was absent from his flock, so I sat obediently yet somewhat disappointed, and half absorbed the word delivered by another. Halfway through service I'd come to the decision to try my luck once more. I'd be back the following Sunday. Three Sundays in a row.

What was wrong with me? Who was this person so intrigued to receive God's word? I'd believed for many years that it was okay to read my Bible on occasion and that was good enough and that my attendance at church was not paramount. So I simply did not attend. I'm sure that this broke my mother's heart. But this too became an unspoken, yet another agreed upon rule that I would faithfully abide in.

When my mother gave her life to Christ, it was a sudden change for our household. I had noticed that all of a sudden she'd started going to church regularly. Then one day she came home and made the announcement, "I got saved at church today. Things are going to change". And change they did! It was not some slow gradual weening from the mother we knew. When she gave her life to Christ, it was like the old mom resigned and another mom applied for the position. She changed! We were no longer able to listen to certain radio stations. No longer allowed to watch certain television shows. She came home that day on a cleaning rampage. She trashed every VHS tape and DVD that we owned. I decided right then and there if 'being saved' meant that I had to become somebody else, I didn't want any parts of it.

That next Sunday I sat in church and was quite pleased to learn that the residing Pastor was present and would deliver the sermon. I sat. I listened. I absorbed. I never noticed that I was breaking the old agreements that I'd set forth. I came back another Sunday and another. I hungered for the word. I wanted to know more. I was eager to learn. I took notes and from those notes, studied upon my return home. A heart that had once held onto so much hurt was being made over. Each Sunday as I sat in church, I was opening up more and more. At the end of every sermon, the Pastor would announce, "The doors of the church are open...", this is when I truly began to feel a very distinct pull. Then there were those services I attended when it felt like the Pastor was speaking directly to me, or the time he said that it doesn't matter what you look like, that you can still accept Christ and the amazing part of that as I looked down at my tattooed arms and within my broken heart is that for the first time, I knew that Christ had already accepted me. Jesus Christ, the son of God, a representation of The Most High in the flesh, why would *He* love me? I am not immensely smart or extremely pretty. Nothing remarkable to behold. On a good day, I'm average at best and that's been good enough for me. The trials and tribulations that I've endured thus far in my life, I've taken in stride. Survival is a way of life that some understand all too well. Giving up has never been an option for me. I simply rolled with the ebb and flow of life with each tide.

A Child is born.

God bless the Child.

November 14, 1979, a young unwed teenager, gave birth to a baby girl. My earliest memory is the sound of incessant beeping and a blinding white light. When I became old enough to understand, my mother told me the story of my birth. There she was, scared. My father nowhere in sight. After much pain and many hours of labor, my mother delivered a non-breathing baby girl. I can only imagine the hurt my mother must have felt. To have carried a child for 9 months. The world watching as her belly grew. Yet she was privy to a more intimate bond. Quickening, the first feelings of movement; sign that the life growing there is truly a living being. As the weeks progressed the strength of each movement did too. How painful it must have been for my mother to not hear me cry my first cry immediately after I was born.

Silence. Without breath a child cannot cry. After a few decades this side of Heaven, I think it's safe to say that I've experienced my fair share of pain and I can truly only imagine the sound that is the breaking of a mothers' heart. On the very same day that she became a parent, she'd know the pain of losing a child. But that fateful day, just like each thereafter, had already been written. This was not the way the story would end. I was to become a survivor, a fighter, a Warrior. I would bear the unthinkable and never think for a moment that it was some miraculous thing that I made it out alive. After much coaxing (the hand of God on my life), I breathed, I cried.

I always thought that my hardships were a normal part of life. Feeling sorry for myself would have been too easy. Someone long ago once told me that we have a choice in all things and that clearly I had subconsciously chosen not to be bitter at the hand Life herself had dealt. As far as I was concerned, I didn't have a choice. Little did I know that my pain had a purpose.

His Plan.

His Purpose.

Bitter. Angry. Mad. Upset. Disappointed. Hurt. Trapped in a chrysalis of unshed agony. My testimony is not about me as your testimony is not about you! Don't be alarmed, but the truth of the matter is that each testimony was created before you and I were conceived. Its purpose is to exalt The Most High; to edify, glorify and magnify His name. It's time to get over those old hurts and ancient pains. Don't take it personal, but even the body you possess was designed on purpose for His purpose. Now talk about a right proper plan. God specializes in everything! He is especially a Master when it comes to timing. When we set aside the desire for our own understanding, our lives become a vacant vessel for God's divine planning.

Ecclesiastes 3:1-11 -- There is a time for everything and a season for every activity under the heavens:

A time to be born and a time to die, a time to plant and a time to uproot, a time to kill and a time to heal, a time to tear down and a time to build, a time to weep and a time to laugh, a time to scatter stones and a time to gather them, a time to embrace and a time to refrain from embracing, a time to search and a time to give up, a time to keep and a time to throw away, a time to tear and a time to mend, a time to be silent and a time to speak, a time to love and a time to hate, a time for war and a time for peace.

What do workers gain from their toil? I have seen the burden God has laid on the human race. He has made everything beautiful in its time. He has also set eternity in the human heart; yet no one can fathom what God has done from beginning to end.

Sunday after Sunday I continued to sever that old tie. My Mother was just as shocked at this turn of event in my life as I was. I can honestly say that the one thing she did not do once she gave her life to Christ, was to force my younger brother and I to accompany her to church. Sure, she invited us and she was upset whenever we declined, but she never made us go. I suppose she felt that no one had pressured her to accept Christ. Her children were now of a certain age. Not so young that we'd go willingly just because she bid it so, and just old enough to make that decision on our own. So she never pressed the issue.

Something you must understand about my upbringing, I wasn't raised by a Mother who took us to Sunday School in our youth. There was no church every 2nd and 4th or 1st and 3rd Sunday. There was 1 momma working 2 jobs, singlehandedly raising us. On occasion there would be a new boyfriend on the scene or the undercurrent of a pungent aroma dimly masked by the burning of incense, lingering thick as shame in the air.

Please forgive my initial feelings in regards to my Mother's newly turned leaf. For a couple of decades, the thought of 'getting saved' brought to mind a very particular archived image of my mother. No more blonde highlights, bright red lipstick, wide leather belts, fun mom. She literally, right before our very eyes, became someone else and the seemingly overnight transformation totally took her children by surprise. And even though she never forced her newfound religion on us, she let it be known that, "Hell is real" and she had no intentions of going there. I took that warning lightly. When my mother gave her life to Christ, I was young, mid-teens. I had time to get right with the Lord, if that's what I chose to do.

So imagine my Mother's surprise as well as delight when she learned I had been attending church regularly ever since that fateful service at her home church. She was pleased to say the least, but I was afraid.

Fear had begun to set in. They say that all (good) things must come to an end. But God's love is eternal, everlasting, never ending. I've been through many phases in my life... The 'bad boy' phase, the 'ripped jeans & short shorts' phase, the 'new tattoo every other month' phase, the 'wild, unruly, disobey everything your mother says', also known as the 'sneak out, stay out, skip school, don't come home for days' or mildly put, the infamous 'teenager' phase. Like my mother before me, I even went through a bit of a 'migration' phase where I was constantly uprooting my little family. This whole 'going to church' thing, was this too just a phase? Would I soon come to my senses and reestablish those old agreements?

Eternal. Everlasting. Never ending. I'm in it for the long haul. God has ordered my every step and each one, even those that at times seemed the furthest from Him, drew me to Him. And now that I'm here, I'm not ever going back.

Change of heart.

Change of mind.

You cannot truthfully receive the word of God and not experience some sort of change! I'm going to church every Sunday. I'm learning about God's unchanging hand. I'm being transformed. I'm eager to know more, be more, do more. Why is it that no one questions a world of sin, but let some brave, unashamed soul confess that they are a new creature in Christ, and everything they do will be scrutinized. So much pressure to be 'perfect'... Can I handle it?

Mark 9:23 – "'If you can?'" said Jesus. "Everything is possible for one who believes.'"

So do I keep it to myself or do I share my excitement? His love is sweeter than honey. I just want to tell the world. But I don't want to offend anyone. I don't want to bore them. I don't want them to look at me differently. What would Jesus do? I believe Jesus would wear the love He has for His Father, like a robe!

Then He'd walk into town and cry out His confession for all the world to witness. He has already done this. Now it's up to a select brave, unashamed few to carry on God's work.

All roads lead home...

Eventually!

The entryway will be narrow, but the Kingdom of God is vast and all of its wondrous lavishness has been promised to those who receive His son Jesus as their Lord & Savior. For me, the path to this point in my life has not been easy and there have been times when it seemed either all uphill with the weight of the world bearing down on my shoulders, or all downhill without a break in sight. I reflect on my birth often because it could have ended there. But the pain that God allows is accompanied by great purpose. All lives unravel at their own pace and on their own paths--freewill guiding and misguiding. Have you ever heard the saying that, "All roads lead home"? And they do. Some routes are quicker than others. Some individuals have always known the way. For others, it may take traveling the scenic, longer, more arduous course before reaching that destination. But I believe in my heart that all roads truly do lead home. Now whether or not you'll be allowed entry once you reach the gate, will depend upon your actions along the way. Here is the road I traveled...

All new life begins with death. I eventually breathed life into my lungs and cried my first tears.

My early years were spent under the watchful eye of my single mother. By the age of 5, a baby brother had joined us, turning the duo into a threesome. My father was a phantom. Bits and pieces, fragments, shards of remembrance lodged themselves in my brain. He became a forgotten face with an unspoken name. I didn't really know him or his wife and their children. It's a hard thing to acknowledge that a parent does not want you. Perhaps this is why my grandparents, my father's mother and father, took up as much time as they could with me. Swooping in to rescue me from the boring humdrum existence that is summer vacation in the country. Too far from the city, not close enough to the beach, wedged somewhere in between. In 'the middle of nowhere' is what the old folks called it. My paternal grandfather was a retired military man and my paternal grandmother had chosen a life of domestic duties. During this time in my life they drove an 18 wheeler. So when I say they swooped, that's truly what I mean. I'd spend summers with my grandparents, traveling and on occasion throughout the course of my early years, I'd be briefly in the presence of my father; the minutes were fleeting and truly momentary. Every Easter his parents sent me a frilly dress; blush pink, sunshine yellow or some other pastel hue of the rainbow. An Easter basket full of goodies would arrive every spring and in the winter, just in time for Christmas, a gingerbread house boasting its sugary goodness was guaranteed Special Delivery at our local post office. Then there was the long awaited school dismissal and my grandparents never missed a summer. And even though they were a few states and at least a few hundred miles away, they never missed a birthday. I miss those days. My mother's mother died long before I reached this age and my mother's father lived about a thousand miles away! But even with the absence of one set of grandparents, my father's parents did everything they could to make sure my childhood was as sugary sweet as the gingerbread houses of my early years.

By the age of 10, I'd become more curious about my father. Who was he? What was he like? Had he forgotten about me? Did he love me? At the end of my 5th grade year, I'd gain access to the source of these and so many more questions. To this day, I don't believe I've received an answer other than, even the pain my 'earthly' father caused had its purpose.

A summer vacation that began with a beloved aunt and a step mother I knew very little about, turned into 3 years of hell. According to my mother, I was 'legally' abducted (*please read and understand the fine print before you sign anything, especially matters pertaining to your children).

My grandfather died that summer and my father molested me for the first time. Over the course of the next few years, what was weekly became daily. Who was he? My father, my abuser. What was he like? The 'loving' but stern, military dad that he was, he doted on his sons, as for me, I can still remember the first time he pried my knees apart in the backseat of his Suburban behind some abandoned building, and the piercing pain of my daddy's penis as he entered his daughter's vagina and rape became forever a part of me. Had he forgotten about me? In the sense that a dad should regard a daughter, yes... In the sense that one treats a lover, no... Did he love me? Does he love me? God will be the judge of that.

My teen years were laced with morbid thoughts. How could I go back to a life of normalcy after all that I'd been through. I did not just endure rape physically; I'd endured it mentally, and now I was expected to 'put the past behind' me, and not talk about what happened. The things that hurt from within are much easier to deal with than unsightly scars, cuts and bruises. It's almost like, if you don't see the pain, it doesn't exist. But it's still there. Sometimes deeper than any physical wound. I was certain that the pain of death would only last a little while compared to the nightmares that had taken over my sleep state. I'd spend hours outside watching the cars pass by, wondering which driver was driving fast enough to end the suffering. All I had to do was just step into the traffic. But I kept silent for my mother's sake. Never fully disclosing the details of the time spent in my fathers' home. And I never told her that I wanted to end my own life. She'd been through enough, so I spared her my hurt. Perhaps it was her who unknowingly kept me from getting too close to the edge. Then again, maybe it was something else keeping me.

This was about the same time that my mother gave her life to Christ. I'd always heard that people often seek Him when they are in the midst of trying times. Maybe the pain I'd endured was too great for my mother to handle alone, so she took it to the One who knows no burden that is too great. The nearer she drew to God, the further I pulled away from her. Tension rose in our home. Mother and daughter became distant strangers and I sought love the way my father taught me, with open legs as opposed to an open heart. A few weeks before my 16th birthday, I found out I was pregnant. My first child would be a son. He was born with Sickle Cell Disease, a lifelong illness. A child is born. Another single mother Another absentee father.

My 20's are a blur. One bad relationship after another. I was the mother of three children before I celebrated my 25th birthday. The arrival of daughters prompted a new era for me. One in which I began to see the error of my ways with men more and more. I didn't want my children, especially my daughters, to become victims of such a sick, sadistic and senseless act as sexual abuse. I could not risk it. It was time to start growing up. So I returned to school and received a Diploma in Early Childhood Care & Education. I entered the workforce and retained employment when my son's illness would permit. Daycares. Head Starts. Childcare facilities. For some strange reason I gravitated towards children. So many parents and caregivers were opting out of their obligation and dismissing their responsibility to keep them safe. I watched and I listened and I searched my heart for the warning signs of neglect and abuse of the children within my care.

Then a spell of unemployment settled itself beside me. My son was in and out of hospitals due to his illness. The social security that I received was barely enough to make ends meet. Three growing children equals three hungry mouths to feed, never mind my own. Food stamps to supplement the supplement income. So many nights I went to bed hungry, but I rested easy knowing that my babies' bellies were full. That is a parent's love.

My 30's thus far have been a great awakening for me. One minute my children were babies and the next they are teenagers and young adults about to embark upon the world on their own. Their upbringing has been a combination of my own struggle to grow up, constant relocating, a parade of those who made good on their promise to be in our lives if only for one night, limited funds, and all the love in my heart. So what, a few men came and went their way. A few loved ones departed from the physical world. I lost jobs. We moved, a lot. My mother and I were on again, off again at odds. I wasn't able to give my children everything they wanted but I did my best to provide most of what they needed, and aside from the trauma inflicted by my biological father during my early years, no significant tragedy occurred in my life. It may seem odd that right in the midst of my happiness, I sought joy.

For Better.

For Worse.

When I stopped looking for love and had vowed that I would never allow sex ever again to rule or ruin my life, my husband came along. It was him who lifted the veil and never looked away when all the broken pieces were revealed. His presence forced me to look back at all the bad that had happened in my life. It was like witnessing a real life tragedy. The journey had been paved with sadness, hurt, shame, abandonment, confusion, abuse. But for the first time I saw the tiny slivers that marred the surface and penetrated through the depths of those ugly truths. There had been bliss, happiness and laughter along the way. The birth of my children despite the struggle to raise them on my own. The health of my son despite his illness. The beautiful friendship between mother and daughter despite the origins of the rocky relationship. The road has been hard and long, but even on rainy days, the sun never stopped shining up ahead. Instead of an ongoing pity party, I pressed forward. One foot in front of the other. Never bitter. Never mad. Never questioning. Never stopping to wonder how I was able to move on.

Now I know... It was the grace of God that kept me then and keeps me still.

Coupled with my husband's love which pales only in comparison to the love of Jesus Christ and God, the journey itself is what brought me to this point. God does not wish to see His people suffer, but what weight does a testimony hold for the one who has never been tested? If it weren't for the bad, I wouldn't have recognized nor appreciated the good.

I appreciate my husband. God designed. God fearing. God sent. I believe The Creator has a divine sense of humor. A sense of humor with infinite timing. He knows exactly where to insert the punchline. My husband hails from a family with a heavy religious background. God laughs here. Of all the men to be my helpmate, He sends the one willing to begin the healing process of my heart. The one willing to salve the pain and soothe the nightmares of my past. The one willing to say, "Look at the good here, and here, and here, and here..." The one who believes in Him! I see the irony. Even funnier is the fact that although it is my husband that comes from a family of Preachers, Ministers and Evangelists, it was I who first took that leap of faith. I who pressed my way through the crowd that fateful day to meet the young, enigmatic Pastor. I who, Sunday after Sunday, sat in church breaking those old agreements. I who first confessed that I was ready to be saved. Encouraged by my husband to do what I knew in my heart to be right. As the head of our household, I sought and took solace in my husband's approval.

Not everyone will understand or support, or even respect your choice to give your life to Jesus Christ. The decision to do so must be for you and you alone. I was lucky to have a husband who understood, supported and respected my choice, so when the decision was made, it was him who stood by my side and he too dedicated his life! That fateful first Sunday marked not only a new calendar year, but a new beginning in our lives!

I believe that no matter what waters you choose to navigate or what direction the undercurrents of life may take you, we all inexplicably wind up in the exact place where we are supposed to be. All roads lead home! I believe that with all my heart and I know that when the breath leaves my body and my time on earth has come to an end, I'll transcend into Heaven byway of the Gatekeeper (Jesus Christ) to be with The Creator (God). I am royalty... The daughter of The Most High King. The legacy of the lineage of The Lord of Lords!

His kingdom is my inheritance, and for that I am glad.

By Fire.

By Water.

After giving our lives to Christ, my husband and I were baptized. The act of being baptized is not to be saved! You are saved once you confess with your mouth that Jesus Christ is the son of God and you believe in your heart that He died for our sins. Being baptized is an outward show to the world that you *are* saved. It's a feeling like none other. Greater than bearing and giving birth to my children. Greater than marrying my best friend. I can only imagine how great it will be in the presence of Him that created me in His own image. Prayerfully I have many more miles to travel before that day comes. I know that there will continue to be trials, troubles and tribulations, but those who are tested in the fire, will emerge from those cleansing waters victorious, with a testimony that is fireproof.

It is...

An Ongoing Battle.

We are each riddled with all sorts of flaws, faults and failures. To err is human nature. We are hopeless, inferior, weak, nothing without Him! Deeply rooted behaviors dwell within us. We are creatures of habit. I can feel myself more and more slipping back into my old ways. Telling myself that I don't have to attend church on a regular basis. I believe in God. I gave my life to Jesus Christ. I got saved. I got baptized. Isn't that enough? A Sunday here and a Sunday there passes by and I find it hard to get myself to the place of worship. But we must remember, companionship on this journey is paramount. I'm still new here. There is so much I don't know and so much more I yearn to know. Is it enough that I got saved? That I got baptized? No! Because this thing is not about me.

Saints, let's remember to keep our eyes on the finish line! Battles continue to wage on, but the war has already been won. We mustn't give up. Never quit. Never stop running. The moment we stop running is the moment we forget what we're even running for.

A Few Personal Afterthoughts

Visiting Dignitary

I'm an alien visiting a foreign land. None of us are natives to this place. We are each simply passing through. Earth may be my birthplace, but Heaven is my birthright. Yes! I am claiming a most divine inheritance. The daughter of The King of all Creation. He has breathed breath into every living thing, even me! That makes me royalty. Hear me now, we are travelers and I recognize that I am simply passing through. Celestial. Extra-terrestrial. This middle ground is not my home.

Clarification

Just because Jesus congregated with sinners, doesn't mean He condoned the things they did. Neither did He condemn the individual. Jesus Christ came to the world to deliver a message so that we could all be saved. In the end, the Messenger, the Messiah, The Son of God, gave His life for us.

I Am His Greatest Design

Science says that we evolved. Religion says that we were created. I believe that each are relevant and depend on one another. My opinion is that, even if we evolved, every living organism needs a point to evolve from—a source of creation. Stars inhabit our day and our night skies. The sun is the largest star of them all; but just as significant are the stars that light up the heavens at night.

Genesis 1:1; "In the beginning, God created the heavens and earth."

Genesis 1:3; "And God said, "Let there be light," and there was light."

Genesis 1:5; "God called the light "day," and the darkness he called "night." And there was evening, and there was morning—the first day."

Genesis 1: 16-18; "God made two great lights—the greater light to govern the day and the lesser light to govern the night. He also made the stars. God set them in the vault of the sky to give light on the earth, to govern the day and the night, and to separate light from darkness. And God saw that it was good."

Stars are a chemical compound of many elements, majorly iron and oxygen. The oldest living star discovered, estimated to be over 14 billion years old, is comprised of a much higher concentration of oxygen than the newer stars that occupy the night sky. Where did the breath that breathed the oxygen of life into that light source come from? Consider this: God's voice is the base & treble behind the Big Bang Theory. The Universe didn't just all of a sudden resolve into a state of existence. I personally refuse to believe that. But that's just me of course.

To Believe... Or Not To Believe

Yesterday. Today. Tomorrow. The world we live in is not so different. There always have been and there will always be, those who believe and those who do not believe. But disbelief does not cause a thing to cease being. It still exists. God is real.

Designed to testify before you were conceived. Your every step brings you closer to Me. You trudge on in aguish despite the hurt and pain. Your tears and tribulations, nary a one in vain. There will be good days but they won't always outweigh the bad. Feelings of defeat will likely be had. You'll want to throw in the towel and give up. But just when you reach the end of your rope and think, "No more, I've had enough"! I'll be there with My arms open wide, welcoming you home. And you'll finally know that you've never been alone. I was there on the darkest day and the longest night. When life took you to it, it was I who brought you through it. That beacon of hope that urges you to carry on. The sunshine, the cloudless day, the rainbow after the storm. I've been there all along. Waiting with open arms for my greatest design to come home.

Dear Reader,

The pages that follow are a place to reflect, a place to write your thoughts. Use the space to inscribe the Bible verses that speak to you. Record your steps as you journey to be in God's presence. We were each designed to testify. Write...

Check out these books by the Author!

Can't Raise No Man—
Single mother. Raising a child. Not just any child. A man child. On her own. Alone... And the world is divided. There are those that say it can be done & there are those that say it can't.— "Oh you're just a woman. You can't raise no man. He need a daddy. Honey, where yo' husband at?" —Who are they to tell me I can't raise no man? We'll show them. {ISBN—9780986100130}

Carnal Sobriety—
When desire becomes addiction, which way do you turn? When every ex-lover is your dealer, how do you break free? Carnal Sobriety—a true story of sexual addiction. {ISBN—9780989678667}

Mojo For Sale: The Art of Encouraging One's Self—
We all need inspiration, motivation and encouragement from time to time, but where can we turn to find it? In Mojo For Sale, we find a wealth of sources each easily within reach. Mojo For Sale—your guide to the inspiration within. {ISBN—9780989678612}

FreedomInk Publishing. Books that entertain, educate, embolden, empower & enlighten...
www.freedomink365.com/the_books

Katandra Jackson Nunnally resides in southeast Georgia with her husband and three children. The CEO of FreedomInk Publishing, spends her time delicately balancing the role of wife, mother, devout Christian, avid reader, lifelong learner, and Author, amongst a host of other things. 'Designed To Testify' is the Author's 7th book.

Connect with the Author:

Instagram--->
http://instagram.com/kat_nunnally/

Facebook--->
https://www.facebook.com/freedomink365ceo

Publisher's website--->
https://www.freedomink365.com/
about_the_publisher

Blog--->
http://freedomink365ceo.wordpress.com/

Twitter---> http://twitter.com/FreedomInk365

Email---> katandra@freedomink365.com